D1622347

SRI CHINMOY

America the Beautiful

Sri Chinmoy (1931-2007) was a poet, author, philosopher, playwright, athlete and musician who dedicated his life to the pursuit of peace and goodwill. The recipient of numerous prizes, awards and honorary doctorates, he has been recognized globally for the simplicity and power of his work. He was born in India and made his home in New York City from April, 1964 until his passing in October, 2007. This is the first paperback of Sri Chinmoy's writing published by Illumine Press and is being released in honor of the 46th anniversary of his arrival in the West.

ILLUMINE GROUP

America the Beautiful

Reflections on Her Past, Present and Future

Compiled from the writings of

SRI CHINMOY

foreword by

DR. JAMES G. BASKER

*Richard Gilder Professor of Literary History,
Barnard College, Columbia University
President, Gilder Lehrman Institute of
American History*

edited by

SANJAY RAWAL

Illumine Press
A Division of Illumine Group, LLC
New York

Praise for the Author

Sri Chinmoy's many contributions to American life and culture have been expressed through teaching, athletics, art, music, poetry and literature. He combines the contemplative traditions of his native India with the dynamism of his adopted America to serve humanity . . . He has dedicated his life to inspiring and serving all those trying to make the world a better place, whether ordinary citizens or those entrusted with the stewardship of a nation.

– Congressman Gary L. Ackerman,
Congressional Record, July 27, 2006

As an accomplished poet, author, artist, musician, athlete and spiritual leader, you have lived your life to the fullest and your achievements are innumerable. Whether it be your service to the UN, the Sri Chinmoy Oneness-Home Peace Run [now the World Harmony Run], the Peace-Blossoms, or your numerous university and literary awards, you have not only been tremendously successful, but inspirational. Your tireless efforts to promote peace around the world is not only exemplary but testimony to the indomitable spirit. May you continue to change the world with your simple message of peace and love.

– Senator Daniel Patrick Moynihan,
April 29, 1999

I congratulate you on the momentous occasion – the 25th anniversary of your coming to the United States of America. I applaud your efforts to achieve world peace. Your activities have touched people in all walks of life in many continents and I wish you continued success.

– Senator Edward M. Kennedy,
June 30, 1989

Your varied activities on behalf of world peace are well known. My prayer is that all citizens of this country and the world will join in quiet, selfless acts of living a life of peace. It will be from this base that lasting peace will spring.

– Senator Claiborne Pell,
November 25, 1992

It was an honor knowing and working with Sri Chinmoy over his many years of dedication by this wonderful philosopher and advocate of world peace. Sri Chinmoy's contribution to the world has enriched all of our lives with his living spirituality and with his dedication to world peace.

– former Congressman Benjamin A. Gilman,
October 9, 2009

Sri Chinmoy has brought forth gifts of beauty and redemption in numerous genres and fields of artistic endeavour. Like Gandhi, like Mother Teresa, like Martin Luther King, Jr., Sri Chinmoy's presence and work among us has enriched all of our lives.

– Professor Charles Johnson, Winner,
National Book Award, November 4, 1995

FIRST ILLUMINE PRESS EDITION JULY, 2010

Bird drawing by Sri Chinmoy. Back cover photo by Adarini Inkei. Edited by Sanjay Rawal.

ISBN 978-0-9824284-6-7

Library of Congress Control Number: 2010925400

Illumine Press
307 7th Ave. Suite 1201
New York, New York 10001
www.illumine.com/press

Printed in the United States of America
10 9 8 7 6 5 4 3 2 1

Contents

Publisher's Note   3

Foreword by Dr. James G. Basker   7

Prologue   15

Awakening   19

Blossoming   37

Reflections   55

Future   71

Notes   95
Biography of Author   101

Publisher's Note

America the Beautiful: Reflections on Her Past, Present and Future is a compilation of nearly 40 years of material authored by Sri Chinmoy in the form of poems, prose, and lectures.

Sri Chinmoy came to the United States as a young man of 32 in 1964 and spent his first two years working at the Indian Consulate on East 64th Street in New York City. Moving from Greenwich Village to Brooklyn to the Upper East Side, and then finally to Queens, Sri Chinmoy took great inspiration from the generosity of spirit and dynamism of New York City and the spiritual awakening of the country.

Even while in India, Sri Chinmoy was a keen student of American history and those great figures who shaped American policy, aspirations, art and psyche. The culmination of twenty years of spiritual discipline at an Ashram, his arrival in America was prompted by an inner call urging him to travel to the West to be of service to sincere spiritual seekers.

In Sri Chinmoy's first decade in the United States he traveled the nation, delivering lectures at august institutions and universities. He also developed treasured friendships with local, regional and national luminaries in many fields who exemplified the Founding Fathers' dedication to freedom and liberty. At the same time, he witnessed firsthand the upheaval of the '60s and then the political and social events of the next four decades.

Sri Chinmoy approached reality from an inner vantage point, concentrating on the essence, soul or potentiality rather than current outer circumstances. Sri Chinmoy always chose to highlight the ultimate divine destiny of humanity. It was his visionary nature that prompted countless messages of support from Senators, Congressmen and other prominent

American leaders over the years. He always encouraged what was good and used that positivity as an illumining force.

This selection is by no means an exhaustive tome of Sri Chinmoy's writings on America, but a mere glimpse at a literary œuvre both vast in its scope and deep in its insight.

Sri Chinmoy loved America. America was his home for 43 years. Her ideals were his aspiration. Her progress and happiness were his goal.

This is the inaugural publication of Illumine Press, released to commemorate the 46th anniverary of Sri Chinmoy's arrival in America on April 13, 1964. We welcome you to this volume and look forward to your response.

– Publisher

America, America, America
Great you are, good you are,
Brave you are, kind you are.
O my America, America
Your Heaven-freedom
Is earth's aspiration choice.
With you, in you
Is God-Hour's Victory-Voice.[1]

– Sri Chinmoy

Foreword

As this extraordinary collection of meditative prose and poetry reveals, Sri Chinmoy loved America. Having come to the United States in 1964, a pivotal time in his own life and that of his adopted country, he expressed his love in a rich and continuous series of reflections that are rooted in American history.

Sri Chinmoy deeply admired the American Founding Fathers – Washington, Jefferson, Adams, Franklin – for their individual virtues and collective achievement.

He salutes in Washington "the indomitable spirit of the general" and praises him for his blend of "high character and majestic will, ... courage and capacity." In leading America to independence and serving as its first president,

Washington became "the Man of Destiny" because "the Divine made him His efficient instrument."

Jefferson, too, made unique and transcendent contributions. Sri Chinmoy calls him "the most divinely talented man of his time," and values him above all for writing the Declaration of Independence. "No other American," he writes, "has done or perhaps will ever do so much for the progress of the American consciousness as Thomas Jefferson."

The Founding of America, in the vision of Sri Chinmoy, was an event not just of national but of global importance. The Founders, he writes, "wanted to show that their liberty was not only for them but for the whole world to use. It was an ideal for the world to embrace."

Elsewhere, drawing on his personal experience and transnational perspective, he writes that the purpose of America is not only its own "illumination and perfection," but "the illumination and perfection of the entire world."

Not that these truths will be universally understood and appreciated. For all his idealism and hope, Sri Chinmoy acknowledges reality. "Those who bring new light into the world will never, never get the appreciation, admiration, adoration and love that they deserve – never!" Nonetheless, he attributes to America a unique importance in world history, both in the past and as its full benefit to humanity unfolds in the future. "The American spirit is America's eagerness to know what the world needs."

Naturally, he also saw in Abraham Lincoln a divinely inspired hero of history. In his admiring and free-flowing poem *Abraham Lincoln*, Sri Chinmoy praises the sixteenth president for upholding equality as "every man's birthright and treasure" and quotes Lincoln's all-important statement that "this nation cannot exist half-slave, half-free."

Lincoln is one of a succession of great Americans who figure in these reflections, including in the 20th century Woodrow Wilson, Franklin Delano Roosevelt, John F. Kennedy, and Dr. Martin Luther King, Jr.

Wilson's great contribution was the League of Nations, which led eventually to the United Nations, a beloved institution in Sri Chinmoy's world view and central to his hope for the future. FDR is given a special place, with Washington, Lincoln, and Kennedy, in the line of greatest American presidents. Martin Luther King of course figured prominently in the life and sorrows of America in the early years when Sri Chinmoy first lived in America, and King's embrace of Gandhi's ideas and spirit no doubt earned him a special place in Sri Chinmoy's feelings. But it is John F. Kennedy who may have touched Sri Chinmoy's heart most profoundly, as we can see in perhaps the most moving of his poems in this volume. He closes the poem with these lines: "Kennedy's life was the world. / Its promise was Kennedy. / Together they breathe through Eternity."

A handful of writers and artists surface again and again in Sri Chinmoy's meditations. The lyricism and free-verse rhythms of his writings are everywhere evocative of Walt Whitman who, together with Emily Dickinson and her "thousands of psychic poems," is revered for his ability to awaken "the consciousness of America."

The great transcendentalists Emerson and Thoreau are also invoked, especially Emerson, who rose so far above parochial or conventional interests that "he studied our Indian Vedas and Upanishads." In part because of their special connections with Lincoln and the transformative events of the mid-19th century, Emerson and Whitman emerge, in Sri Chinmoy's view, as the "twin-souls of the Truth." Among others who appear at different times in his wide-ranging reflections are figures as various as Thomas Paine, Jawaharlal Nehru, Norman Rockwell, Pablo Casals, and Daniel Patrick Moynihan.

Ultimately Sri Chinmoy's vision, centered on America, is one of hope. The birth of America and its issuance of the Declaration of Independence fundamentally changed the world's trajectory.

"The American Declaration of Independence had the pioneer vision of faith, dignity and humanity's basic needs: equal rights, justice, and freedom." Later came the United Nations Charter, which joined the Declaration "like two close friends walking along the same road . . . [toward] the goal of world peace and satisfaction."

Sri Chinmoy is not naïve. Americans can sometimes be "complacent" and "America has bad qualities, true," he observes, "but American principles are absolutely divine." It is on the level of ideals and spiritual purpose that he is most hopeful about the future. "The next two hundred years will see the manifestation of the soul's qualities of America."

America's material wealth is only a stage in its continuing development. Turning to address America directly, Sri Chinmoy notes that an important "achievement of yours has been to build up the material basis for the coming great age of spirituality." Thus, says Sri Chinmoy, the key is a certain generosity of spirit in America: "You live not for yourself alone. You live for freedom and for those who share your love for it."

Every reader, whether American or any other nationality, will be moved by Sri Chinmoy's reflections in *America the Beautiful*. Through these writings, he takes his own place in the history and literature of America, while also shining a light into the future of our country and of the emerging global community.

– James G. Basker

*Richard Gilder Professor of Literary History,
Barnard College, Columbia University
President, Gilder Lehrman Institute of
American History*

Prologue

What is the American spirit?

The American spirit is America's eagerness to know what the world needs.[2]

∞

What does America claim?

A colossal preparation: not only for its own illumination and perfection but for the illumination and perfection of the entire world.[3]

∞

America's mind believes in the theory of give and take; therefore, America is great. America's heart believes in the theory of give, just give; therefore, America is good.[4]

∞

The difference between America's greatness and America's goodness is this: America's greatness silences the world and then beckons the world; America's goodness accelerates the world and then elevates the world.[5]

∞

The soul of America, like a child, is growing, glowing, developing, illumining and fulfilling. It is a soul that is most progressive and most striking.[6]

∞

America's matchless contribution shall be her supreme universal friendship in which the family of nations will see beckoning hands, oneness-satisfaction and perfection-manifestation.[7]

∞

In the Supreme Pilot's scheme of things the United States is going to play the role not so much of leadership as of friendship, nay, brotherhood, in mankind's evolution. And evolution is another name for mankind's spiritual development.[8]

∞

America's goal, like the goal of all the nations and human beings, is always in the process of self-transcendence. There is no fixed goal. America's main goal is a flood of satisfaction, inner and outer. This satisfaction has undoubtedly been achieved to a certain extent. But since everything is progressing and evolving, America's goal is an ever-loving, ever-illumining and fulfilling goal of continuous self-transcendence.[9]

Awakening

Who is a patriot? A patriot is he who loves his country dearly. A patriot is he who loves his country more than he loves his own life. A patriot is he who intuitively feels and infallibly knows that there is nothing and there can be nothing as significant as his own country. A patriot is he who honours and treasures his soul's earthbound and Heaven-descending vision. A patriot is he who fulfils devotedly and untiringly the supreme promise to God, the Absolute Supreme, which he made while he was in the realm of the soul, before entering into the earth-arena. A patriot is he who has discovered the true truth that Heaven is in no way superior to earth.[10]

∞

What is true patriotism? True patriotism is not something that declares war in order to prove its supremacy. True patriotism is not unlit, impure self-assertion. True patriotism is one's genuine love of one's country. True patriotism is loving what one already has. To be precise, true patriotism is real love for what God has already given us out of His infinite Bounty. True patriotism realises the undeniable fact that an individual patriot and his country are but pure instruments of the Absolute Supreme.[11]

∞

Patriots are those who have helped their country and elevated its consciousness so that the reality of their country has widened. There have been many American patriots in the past and there will be many more. The Supreme had a special vision for the soul of America and He revealed it first through the Founding Fathers. The Founding Fathers were definitely spiritually illumined.[12]

∞

The American patriots were great not because they felt that it was beneath their dignity to remain under the jurisdiction of the British, but because they felt that deep within them they had some truly divine spiritual qualities which could easily be brought to the fore. And when these divine qualities were brought to the fore, they felt that not only would they derive infinite benefit and profit from them, but that the whole world would derive benefit. [13]

∞

To destroy a country we need power. This power is undivine, unillumined and ill-founded. To love a country we need a great power. This great power is our pure and constant concern for our country. To serve a country devotedly and untiringly we need a greater power. This greater power is our intuitive and self-offering psychic light.

To claim all nations as our very own, one and inseparable, we need the greatest power. This power is the all-illumining, all-immortalising, all-fulfilling God-Power, which is always crying and trying, trying and crying, to come to the fore from the inmost recesses of our heart. [14]

∞

We are walking along the road of Eternity with a divine, unending, ceaseless and birthless life to manifest the divinity within us. We have to offer to our country what we have: love, sacrifice and the feeling of oneness. The moment we have offered to our country our unalloyed love and pure sacrifice, and have established our inseparable oneness with the soul of our country, to our wide surprise we see that our country has already immortalised us. For our country has chosen us out of millions, billions and trillions of souls to take birth on her shores. Our country has played her role long before we thought of offering something to our country. What we offer to our country is, at best, an iota of love, whereas our country has already inundated us with boundless love. This is the love our country has already achieved and received from the Absolute Supreme.[15]

∞

Patriotism can achieve for a country the message of oneness, the message of satisfaction, the message of human perfection and God-manifestation.

The country is the mother. In order for the mother to be pleased and fulfilled, she has to be given the full opportunity to feed her children unreservedly. The mother gets this opportunity when the children want from her what she has: her love, her concern, her blessing, her compassion, her sympathy, her feeling of oneness. A patriot can offer his need to the mother country. When he tells his country what he needs, the country gets the opportunity to fulfil it.

Again, when a patriot becomes a real lover of his country, then his love enters into the country. First he cries for love from his country and then he gives the country his own love. When he feels he has no love, he cries for the mother to give him love. Then, when the mother gives love to him, he feels that he has abundant love and he offers it back to his country. When love of country and love from country are simultaneous, the message of oneness, the message of satisfaction, the message of human perfection and God-manifestation can dawn.[16]

∞

Patriotism is self-giving and self-expansion based on your conscious oneness with all consciousness, your inseparable oneness with all. That is the meaning of patriotism in the spiritual sense.[17]

∞

The self-giving of the Founding Fathers was the wish not merely to come out from under the British yoke, but for something higher and deeper. True, first they had to be free from British authority, leadership and guidance. But they had something deeper in the inmost recesses of their hearts that they wanted to express, a higher truth that they wanted to manifest. They wanted to show that their liberty was not only for them to use but for the whole world to use. It was an ideal for the world to embrace, a real ideal in human progress that would stand among humanity's ultimate achievements.[18]

∞

England said to America, "Yours is not revolution but mental confusion." America said to England, "Thank you for your self-styled wisdom."

The world said to America, "America, yours is not revolution but evolution – not only your evolution but the evolution of the world, too." America said to the world, "I love you for your God-ordained encouragement and inspiration."[19]

∞

America's independence, humanity's self-awareness and Divinity's self-transcendence were one, inseparably one.[20]

∞

The light always has to be embodied by great and noble individuals.[21]

∞

The soul of America is extremely fond of patriotism and proud of patriotism because it was the patriotic feeling of some brave, divine human beings that brought about liberty in America. America's soul was in bondage. Its soul, its life of reality, could not come to the fore in the country as a whole. But there came a time when a few heroic divine soldiers felt the necessity of liberating their country. The soul of America came forward to offer its own light and delight to these brave souls. It got the opportunity to inject the feeling of patriotism into these few selected children of America so that they could be true and humble instruments of God and please God according to their capacity, their understanding and their inner and outer awakening.[22]

∞

Victory in the War of Independence is the foundation stone of American nationality. [23]

∞

The American patriots were very noble souls. They never said they desired leadership, but God was moulding them for something. In their case, the word 'God' was not uttered, but they spoke about 'truth'. Patriotism, if it is carried out properly, is truth. India's greatest patriot, Mahatma Gandhi, said God and truth are the same. So, in the case of America, truth was the sole motivating force. But you have to know that practically every American president has used the term 'Almighty Father' in their inaugural addresses. The Almighty Father played His role in silence and in action in and through the leaders of America.[24]

∞

George Washington was the father of the American nation. He was the son of peace and the brother of self-giving.[25]

∞

George Washington, you and you alone were America's supreme need and divine choice to lead your country to victory!

You offered your country the smile of victory's freedom-dawn.

Victory's sun shone on the life and soul of America. And that sun blessed you, embraced you and treasured you.[26]

∞

I salute the indomitable spirit of the General in you. I bow to the peerless wisdom of the

President in you. I take endless pride in the Father of the Nation in you.

You have always been a true lover of peace. You have always valued peace infinitely more than anything else. Your country needed you to fight for her. Your country needed you to liberate her from bondage-night. You surrendered your own will to our country's will. Under your supreme leadership your country won the war.

Then your country needed you desperately to build an undivided nation. Your country needed your guidance inimitable. You were the first and last president to be everybody's choice. Many succeeded you, but you, with your lofty ideals, will be their pole star.[27]

∞

George Washington

> A divinely inspired dream, daring and
>   desperate;
> A surprise that made history:
> A farmer's son founds the New World.

"Inferior endowment from nature,"
    he thought of himself.
But the Divine made him His efficient
    instrument.
High character and majestic will
Powerfully blended with courage and
    capacity:
Thus stood forth the Man of the Hour,
The Man of Destiny, the Man of God.

And from his mighty dream mightily
    executed
Burst forth a new free world,
Destined to be the hope and defence
Of more free worlds to be.

Victory in the War of Independence:
England lost to her own offspring.

England won for herself a mightier friend.
A new era heralded,
A new shattering blow
Struck at man's domination over man:
Independence the first step to unity,
And unity, one Truth of God.

George Washington, first to embody
    America's hope,
First in inspiration, first in confidence,
First in war, first in victory,
First in conquering the heart of his nation,
First to envisage a federation of states,
Single, powerful, united, whole.[28]

∞

The essential qualities of Thomas Jefferson
were clarity, luminosity and vastness. Clarity,
luminosity and vastness – these the Declaration
of Independence embodies. Jefferson was the
most divinely talented man of his time. He
covered quite a few fields in every walk of life,
and he went a considerable distance in each. In
his case mind, body, vital, heart – everything –
went together. This moment he was a musician
next moment he was a sculptor; this moment
he was a man of brain, next moment he was
a physical, earthly labourer. God gave him
capacities in many walks of life and he used
them well. One book speaks about Jefferson as
"the happiest man." To become the happiest
man is the most difficult thing on earth – and
that he was.[29]

∞

Unfortunately, Jefferson came long before the world, especially America, was prepared for his beautiful and powerful wisdom-light. Always prophets come at least one minute before the world is able to appreciate them. When they are here, they are not accepted. They have such wisdom, but they are not taken seriously. Only afterwards does the world accept and appreciate them.[30]

∞

Thomas Jefferson never was and perhaps never will be appreciated in the way God wanted him to be appreciated because gratitude was not, is not and never will be born in this world. No other president, no other American, has done or perhaps will ever do so much for the progress of the American consciousness as Thomas Jefferson has done. Countries other than America that have developed inner vision will appreciate Jefferson much more than America.

Those who bring new light into the world never, never get the appreciation, admiration, adoration and love that they deserve – never! This will never happen, because the kind of gratitude that is worthy of their light and their vision has not been born and never will be born on earth.

Jefferson's vision elevated the consciousness of the world in the twinkling of an eye. The light that he wanted to show his country and the light that he wanted his country to bring forward was so badly misunderstood! He never received the appreciation that he so rightly deserved and he will never get it, because humanity does not have that kind of gratitude.[31]

∞

Thomas Jefferson, for your extraordinary service to your country, you would have been known as a great man. But for your offering of your Independence-Declaration, you are known as a good man, a God-messenger, a Vision-son of God.[32]

∞

Washington lives at one place – in the heart of America. Jefferson lives at three places – in the heart, head and eyes of America. The heart represents the feelings, the head represents the intellect and the eyes represent the vision.

When we think of Washington, we think only of the mission that he had to fulfil. He had to do his duty by his country. This was not his self-imposed duty. It was a duty cast upon him by his mother and others who begged him to become the leader of the nation. But when we think of Jefferson, vision and mission go together. He saw the inner promise of America and he was able to reveal it.

When we look at Washington, we see his power aspect. He played the role of a supreme hero and defeated the British in battle. His was the power not to illumine others but to conquer them. When we look at Jefferson, we see his light aspect. Unlike Washington, he did not have to show his heroism. His role was to stabilise the country by spreading his light. In his case, it was his inner vision or light that conquered the hearts of others.

Washington's message was for America. It did not extend beyond the boundaries of his country. His aim was to expel the British and he assumed responsibility for accomplishing this feat. Jefferson's message was for the whole world. When he wrote, he did not specify any country. His words are applicable to the entire humanity. The source of Jefferson's vision was inner light. This light spread from Jefferson's heart to his country and then to the world at large.

Washington was like a small circle that grew larger and larger as his power expanded. Jefferson was not like a circle. His light was not confined. It simply permeated the world wherever it could, according to the receptivity of the individuals.

When Washington was playing the role of a dynamic hero, Jefferson was not in the picture. Jefferson came afterwards to help the young nation make progress. He said, "We have thrown the British out of our country, but it is not enough just to defeat our enemies. If we want to make progress and go ahead, then we have to bring forward the inner light." Jefferson's vision came as the light that America needed in order to become fully mature. Jefferson's vision came as the light that the whole world needs in order to become divinely perfect.[33]

∞

Thomas Jefferson's vision was the Declaration of Independence. But it is not Jefferson's vision alone. Many people saw the reality. It was the vision of that era, the vision of all who surrounded Jefferson. You can call it the vision of Washington, Adams, Franklin, Paine and others. Again, the sense of sacrifice of all those who fought for this country in those days – no matter how little or how much – deserves our special attention.[34]

∞

Who could have envisaged that the thirteen colonies would one day develop into such a powerful country – fifty states standing indivisible, united by none other than the Hand of the Supreme Being? For the United States, the heart-throbbing and life-illumining song 'united' had its birthless and deathless origin in the hearts of the great Americans whose names are synonymous with the lofty principles of liberty, justice and oneness. The founder of the nation, George Washington; the vision-luminary, Thomas Jefferson; the wisdom-sun, Benjamin Franklin; and the tireless fighter, John Adams: these powerful luminaries, along with others, bravely dreamt of unity for the thirteen colonies.[35]

Blossoming

We see another wave of patriotism when President Abraham Lincoln came to office. [36]

∞

Lincoln was a seeker in the pure sense of the term. God gave him a magnanimous heart. Emerson said of him, "His heart was as great as the world, but there was no room in it to hold a wrong."

When we become a seeker, we try to have a heart as vast as the world itself, or try to have a heart even vaster than the world. In this vast heart, a real seeker does not see the ignorance of the world as belonging to others. The heart of a true seeker sees the imperfections, limitations and bondage of others as its very own. Emerson says Lincoln's heart did not hold a wrong, but I wish to say that his heart did not hold a wrong of his own. His heart did hold the wrongs of millions and billions of human beings, and he accepted these wrongs of others as his very own – not with a sense of pride, but with a sense of oneness. [37]

∞

Abraham Lincoln

Born under no lucky star,
But dynamic in his dreams,
He fought his way to Luck:
"From log cabin to White House."

No soul on earth supreme over another –
Equality every man's birthright and
     treasure –
Black and white, brown and red
Make no difference –
This nation cannot exist half-slave, half-free:
From his voice these bold truths rang out.

He had the gift to dream of union,
The courage and capacity to fight,
The confidence to win,
The patience that knew no flagging.
Faith in God's Justice was his stamina,
Faith in God was his might.

Natural the affinity of vision-luminous
    souls,
So Emerson could say of Lincoln:
"His heart was as great as the world,
But there was no room in it to hold a
    wrong."

"Force is all-conquering,
But its victories are short-lived."
Love is all-conquering,
And its victories live on forever.

What is really important?
Are we God's or is God ours?
The idealist in Lincoln reveals:
"We trust, Sir, that God is on our side.
It is more important to know
That we are on God's side." [38]

∞

With President Woodrow Wilson, we notice another wave of patriotism. [39] Wilson was the chief architect of the organisation known as the League of Nations, which was potentially a step towards human unity. "Unless America takes part in this treaty," Wilson was firmly convinced, "the world is going to lose heart. I cannot too often repeat to you how deep the impression made upon me on the other side of [the] water is that this was the nation upon which the whole world depended to hold the scales of justice even. If we fail them, God help the world! Then despair will ensue." [40]

∞

It was the vision of an American to have the League of Nations, but the ignorance of America did not accept this vision. It was not supported by America. As an American, Wilson was listened to, admired and appreciated by many, many countries because he saw the light. But the members of his own family were not accepting his light. Still, it was not all darkness and we see another wave of patriotism at that time. And the League of Nations grew into the United Nations. [41]

∞

President Franklin D. Roosevelt. He was elected for an unprecedented four terms. There was tremendous, tremendous light in President Roosevelt. [42]

∞

O man of lofty ideals, O hero-warrior, O prophet of the world-illumining dawn, we soulfully salute you! [43]

∞

The supremacy of your soul's will-power over your body's revolt, your physical paralysis, was unparalleled. Your very existence was a stranger to fear. Your indomitable courage was far beyond the flight of our wildest imagination. It was your heart's wisdom-light that so lovingly and convincingly taught the entire world: "The only thing we have to fear is fear itself." Indeed, the vision-light of this loftiest message can illumine the length and breadth of the world.

President Roosevelt, the embodiment of your vision-height and action-power will always be treasured by the freedom-loving and peace-spreading world. [44]

∞

O great, good, illumining, inspiring and fulfilling soul, to you we bow. [45]

∞

President John Fitzgerald Kennedy. There have been so many undivine stories about his personal life, but this is all nonsense. We have to see Kennedy's vision, his real vision. Kennedy's soul went very high and very deep. He died quite young; that is why his soul's light did not manifest fully in the outer life. But the patriotism in his inner life is bound to manifest in the course of time. The light that his soul has will again try to manifest on earth through a different form. He will be known as somebody else, but it will be the same soul. Again, the light that an individual embodies need not remain dormant in him until he comes back to earth again. His light can operate through his dear ones or through those who are not near or dear but who have the same principles. They may not even be

American, but they may carry Kennedy's illustrious vision. [46]

∞

John Fitzgerald Kennedy: President of America, prince of high idealism, freedom incarnate, helper of humanity. [47]

∞

If America wants to be friends with all the world, who can be her enemy? Says her mouthpiece, President Kennedy:

"We are not against any man, or any nation, or any system, except as it is hostile to freedom."

It seems that in Kennedy's dictionary there are two complementary words which enrich and fulfil the sense of each other and constitute together the master formula of the language: freedom and peace.

"We will make clear that America's enduring concern is for both peace and freedom; that we are anxious to live in harmony with the Russian

*people; that we seek no conquests, no satellites,
no riches; that we seek only the day when 'nation
shall not lift up sword against nation, neither
shall they learn war any more.' "*

True, poverty and ignorance are man's bitter
foes. But to replace poverty by affluence
and ignorance by knowledge is not enough.
Material success is not all. The quest of the
spirit is of vital importance. "For the first
time," said Kennedy, "we have the capacity to
strike off the remaining bonds of poverty and
ignorance, to free our people for the spiritual
and intellectual fulfilment which has always
been the goal of our civilization."

President Kennedy was, as it were, the lineal
descendant of the American nation's tradi-
tional leadership. As George Washington was
the father of the United States, as Abraham
Lincoln was its saviour, as Franklin D.
Roosevelt was the voice of America, even so,
John F. Kennedy was the noble defender of
world freedom and world peace. [48]

∞

John Fitzgerald Kennedy

> Kennedy is unique.
> Why?
> God kindled him with His Dream.
> On him God showered
> His Blessings divine,
> Thickly,
> Lavishly,
> Significantly.
>
> Kennedy is unique.
> Why?
> God threw on him
> The burden of the world at large,
> Smilingly,
> Consciously,
> Inevitably.
>
> Kennedy is unique.
> Why?
> His soul visioned Tomorrow's Dawn,
> Far beyond the flight of imagination,
> Far above the strongest investigation,
> Deep within the core of transformation.

Kennedy is unique.
Why?
He pined with his bleeding heart
To free the world
From the spiked wounds of life.
This eyeless earth of ours
Will burst into glorious bloom:
He saw this diamond truth,
While dreaming,
Struggling,
Daring. [49]

∞

Never was he alone.
Tragedy and sovereignty,
Catastrophe and victory,
Freely in him were grown.

Never was he alone.
God's bright Promise and Bliss,
Earth's wild ignorance and her kiss,
Lavishly in him were grown. [50]

∞

Alone he stood
    Above all storms of life.
He stood alone
    To challenge pain and strife.
Alone he stood
    To feed a blooming race.
He stood alone
    To change earth's tearful face. [51]

∞

Kennedy, Kennedy, Kennedy, President
    Kennedy:
A mystic name that floats in the ether,
A giant name that swims in the sea of souls,
A dynamic name that stabs through
    human fears.

Kennedy, Kennedy, Kennedy, President
    Kennedy:
A name that drinks God's Nectar of Love,
A name that dances on man's hallowed
    thoughts,
A name of kindled hope below,
Above. [52]

∞

Kennedy's hope was the world.
Its hope was Kennedy.
Kennedy's life was the world.
Its promise was Kennedy.
Together they breathe through Eternity. [53]

∞

Dr. Martin Luther King, Jr. introduced the principle of non-violence to his brothers and sisters who were struggling for equal rights in all spheres of life. His momentous words were:

"I believe that unarmed truth and unconditional love will have the final word in reality." [54]

∞

He was very pure in mind and heart. He was a lover: a lover not only of his race but a lover of all mankind.[55]

∞

His heart was so broad, so great, so magnanimous, and this gave him a most sincere feeling of absolute oneness with everyone. This is what made him so divinely great. [56]

∞

Martin Luther King, beloved king of the heart-world, unhorizoned vision of the mind-world, hero-warrior of the vital-world, life-sacrificer of the body-world, to you my aspiration-dedication-life bows. [57]

∞

In America, the Absolute Supreme chose you to be His unparalleled student, to love divinely the soul of His Creation and to serve unreservedly the body of His Creation. [58]

∞

Many American poets are patriotic heroes just because their inner experiences have awakened and illumined and added to America's consciousness. One may think Walt Whitman's poems are vital, but they are from the dynamic vital, not the aggressive vital. In his poems, he wanted to say, "Do not discard the body-consciousness; value it. The body is not all barren: It is only something for us to utilise. The other side of the body is the soul." He urged humanity to see that inside the body there is also reality. From his body-consciousness he has awakened the consciousness of America. [59]

∞

Whitman is nature. Whitman is vastness. Whitman is all inspiration. Solid and subtle, he is the body and soul of poetry that peers into Truth. His *Leaves of Grass* reveals the depth of his insight and the wideness of his outlook. His determined and forceful personality shines through these poems, which he called "New World songs, and an epic of Democracy."

When the wind and storm of today brings in the golden tomorrow, Whitman will shine forth, haloed in a new glory on the new horizon. His poems and his nation's consciousness are inseparable. A man's poems must always be an absolute reflection of his character and personality. And Whitman is no exception. [60]

∞

Whitman's vision of the oneness of everything and in everything compels him to reveal:

> *"O my soul! If I realise you I have satisfaction.*
> *Animals and vegetables! If I realise you I*
> *   have satisfaction.*
> *Laws of the earth and air! If I realise you I*
> *   have satisfaction."*

Born ahead of his time, Whitman pointed his nation and the world to the path of tomorrow. And, by the Grace of the Supreme, the dawn-rays of tomorrow have already become visible, however faintly, on today's horizon. [61]

∞

Emerson and Whitman are twin-souls of the Truth: Emerson, soft, sweet and luminous; and Whitman, dynamically fronting the Reality which is manifesting to an ever-increasing extent. Fellow-pilgrims on their way to the Home of God, the culmination of today's world, they march in stupendous glory. [62]

∞

Ralph Waldo Emerson also offered most significant service, not only to America but to the whole world. Emerson had an illumined mind. Very few souls as illumined as Emerson have come into the world. Emerson had light in abundant measure. With his illumined mind he served his country and the world. [63]

∞

Emerson received his light, his ideas, from a very old tradition: the Upanishadic teachings. It was not stealing; it came from within, his own inner cry. [64]

∞

America, the fairest land of freedom, opportunity and progress, inspired in Emerson the thought that his countrymen should utilise all her divine gifts to strive for the most divine aims of life. Indeed, America will gain her true stature when she lives up to her philosopher-son's towering aspirations. [65]

∞

Happily, two great contemporaries, Lincoln and Emerson, offer an historic example of mutual appreciation. During the ever-memorable Civil War in America, it was Emerson's inspiration that offered: "the best and the bravest words." He fully supported President Lincoln in his mighty undertaking, and addressed him as: "the protector of American freedom."

Neither could the President remain silent. He honoured the seer in Emerson with his warm appreciation: "The prophet of American faith." [66]

∞

Emily Dickinson wrote thousands of psychic poems. One short poem of hers is enough to give sweet feelings and bring to the fore divine qualities of the soul. [67]

∞

Henry David Thoreau was also a great soul. His vision encompassed the overall experience of reality. [68]

∞

Norman Rockwell not only saw America's simplicity-life and America's happiness-heart, but he also became simplicity and happiness in the purest sense of the term. [69]

∞

America's vastness the world knows. America's oneness only a soul like Norman Rockwell could feel. We, the seekers, shall always feel in him America's oneness-loving life and America's satisfaction-distributing heart. Norman Rockwell embodies the reality's revealed dream. [70]

Reflections

Because of her high ideals, America really did deserve her independence. Also, I wish to say that it usually takes a long time to make the progress America has made. For America to take only a few hundred years to reach her present level of advancement is like doing it in the twinkling of an eye. If any country makes progress, it is for the world's benefit, for other countries as well. [71]

∞

America has bad qualities, true, but American principles are absolutely divine.

Unfortunately, as has happened in other countries, a kind of complacent feeling has entered into Americans; they want to be satisfied with what they have and do not want to go farther. But they should move ahead and strive for a higher consciousness. The goal is not static. [72]

∞

America can run at top speed or it can go slowly and steadily. If it has a complacent feeling and does not want to run fast, then, of course, let it rest. While it is taking rest, there will obviously be a lack of patriotic feelings in the nation. When we reach a certain goal, we think that is the end, but each goal is only the starting point for a higher goal.

Some may blame the young generation for America's lack of aspiration, but actually it depends on human beings of all ages. If we blame the young, then we have to blame their parents and their elders as well. It is not true that a hundred years ago all Americans were absolutely pure, divine and spiritual and that all of a sudden in this century everybody has become undivine. The world is progressing, the world is evolving, but sometimes there are obstructions on the way. When you are running fast, sometimes you become tired and exhausted, and your speed decreases. Instead of speaking of the young generation and the old generation, let us regard both genera- tions as a single human being who is running. At times, he is running at top speed and at times he is running slowly, with the speed of an Indian bullock cart; but even then he is still proceeding along the road. He is either walking or marching or running very fast. So if we see a lack of aspiration right now, then we can say that that person is not running his fastest. He is moving very slowly because he is tired.

We have to know that aspiration is a very vast, complicated subject. Aspiration can be directed towards God-realisation. Industrial progress can also be an object of aspiration. Material progress – not luxury or indulgence but, let us say, scientific progress and discov- ery – is based on aspiration. Twentieth century scientists discovered so many things that the scientists of the eighteenth century had not discovered. So, in that sense the progress that America has made is most praiseworthy.

We have to consider aspiration in all phases of life, not just spirituality. [73]

∞

For the last several decades, the aspiration of young people in America has far surpassed the aspiration of their elders. If anyone says that lack of aspiration is to be blamed on young people, to be very frank with you, I wish to say that the young ones whom I have observed have shown much more aspiration than their parents and superiors. If you examine the spiritual evolution of America, you will see that it is the young generation that is leading it.

When the inner call came, the young generation listened to it. It is the aspiration from the young generation that has kept the banner of America's spiritual life flying. [74]

∞

For the young generation, anything new is good. The young dare to see the face of the new. True, newness need not always mean goodness; but neither can we say that newness is always bad. It is the strength of the young generation that is making America become really spiritual. The young have made mistakes, but they are coming out of their mistakes. Some of them have already come out of their mistakes and now they are turning towards the light. [75]

∞

Previously a soulful promise reigned supreme; now a fruitful hope reigns supreme. The spirit at that time was promise; now it has become hope. The spirit of the past was the discovery of inner adamantine will to fight against bondage. The present spirit is the aspiration for God-manifestation plus the aspiration to become humanity's brother, humanity's selfless lover and divinity's constant server.[76]

∞

How can America afford
To ignore world-problems
When God, out of His infinite Bounty,
Has given America
A heart similar to His own? [77]

∞

The rest of the world needs America, not because America is great but because America is willing – at times conditionally, but always unreservedly. [78]

∞

America's special strength
Lies not in frightening the weak
And challenging the strong,
But in strengthening the weak
And
Illumining the strong. [79]

∞

I hear America singing.
I must say,
America's voice is loud;
America's voice is good,
And soul-stirring, too.

I see America dancing.
I must say,
Although America's dance
Wants to illumine the world,
It ends by frightening the world

Not only beyond the world-imagination,
But
Beyond her own loftiest imagination, too. [80]

∞

America can serve the world most provided
America feels that the service it renders to the
community of nations is nothing but its own
illumining and self-fulfilling expansion. [81]

∞

*"One should not come to America for the first
time!"*

  – Jawaharlal Nehru

O non-Americans, the heart and soul of
America are welcoming you. Come, with
your openness-heart, to be inseparably one
with America's ascending heart of hope and
manifesting soul of promise. [82]

∞

American citizens can learn to love their country more by realising the supreme fact that there is no difference between true love of one's country and true love of God. One's country is nothing short of God's concentrated creation. [83]

∞

The soul of America is satisfied, but since there is no end to outer and inner progress, the soul of America could be more satisfied if America cared more devotedly for its outer and inner progress. [84]

∞

You can love America much more sincerely and soulfully provided you feel that America is not a vast piece of land and a machine-driven country, but a life-illumining, love-fulfilling and peace-spreading country. [85]

∞

Smile, America, my America,
Smile!
Why do you weep, why do you cry?
The world's volley of criticism

Need not curse the real in you
And
It cannot curse the real in you.
Smile, America!
Run and jump!
Fly!
Achieve and become!
Smile, America, smile! [86]

∞

American leaders can best foster true patriotism only when they themselves are true patriots – not in name or word, but in action. True
patriotism is self-giving for a higher and nobler
cause. When the American leaders become
truly self-giving at every moment, then
whatever they do and say for their country
will be for the betterment and improvement
of their country and not for the aggrandise-
ment of their own egos, either consciously,
subconsciously or unconsciously. At this time,
American leaders without fail will foster true
patriotism in others. Patriotism in the purest
sense of the term will be injected into the heart
of the entire American nation.

For, every action of theirs will be a conscious, constant self-giving to expand, enlarge and illumine the consciousness of America for America's sake and not for the glorification of any individual. [87]

∞

One does not have to be one hundred percent behind the government in order to become a patriot. We have to know that it is not the government that we want to govern our country; it is the collective aspiration that will guide the country. If the government fails in fulfilling our aspiration, then we shall not look up to the government to guide us. It is the real in us that will guide the nation. By dint of fate, some individuals in the government are ruling the body of the country. But they are not ruling the heart of the country. As individuals, we are given ample opportunities to illumine the fate of the country. When people in authority misuse their power, eventually they are dethroned. History bears witness to this fact; it bears witness to the fact that hundreds of kings, potentates, presidents and statesmen have all had to come down from the highest height because of their misuse of power.

On your part, as a seeker, you have to create aspiration and inspiration in those of your countrymen who do not subscribe to the views of the government. It is not that you are rebelling against the government, but only that you have seen a higher light and you are offering your higher light in a spiritual way. You are offering it, not with any animosity or antagonistic feeling, but with the higher thought that you can better the consciousness of your country, and with that you are embarking on this new divine project. [88]

∞

Undoubtedly, patriotic feelings in the past were infinitely stronger than what you observe now. [89]

∞

In the days of the American Revolution, patriotism was something living. It was essential, like breathing air. But now patriotism – not only in America but all over the world – has become a mere word. [90]

∞

The American patriots of the past felt that life and patriotism were inseparable. They felt that patriotism was the manifestation of life's freedom, that it was the only way to love one's country. And they did not expect anything from the country. They only wanted to give what they had and what they were. Now, not only in America, but everywhere, everybody wants to take from their country. Nobody wants to give to their country. President Kennedy said: "Ask not what your country can do for you, ask what you can do for your country." At every moment we expect from our country, but what have we done for it? Our forefathers did not expect anything from their country. [91]

∞

God is really on the side of that particular nation that says it is on God's side. If a nation can sincerely say that it does not want God to be on its side, but that it wants to be on God's side, then God is definitely on that side. If a nation begs God to be on its side, it is because of ego and desire. But if a nation says, "I am always eager to be on Your side, whatever side

You take," then immediately God has to be on that nation's side. [92]

∞

You can best regain the nobility and wisdom of the Founding Fathers in America by meditating on the independence-spirit of America, which was treasured not only by earth's aspiration but also by Heaven's illumination.[93]

∞

America's hope, America's promise and America's freedom – these three qualities America can transmit to the world-body today provided America does not claim them as her own personal achievements, but as compassionate boons from Above, from the Almighty Father. [94]

∞

No matter what ultra-modern science has made of America, no matter what the modern intellectual giants have made of America, in the depths of America's heart and life there shall always dwell three virtues: simplicity – a childlike simplicity; happiness – a child's happiness; and satisfaction – a child's constantly blossoming satisfaction that comes when America becomes and offers to the world what the child in it has.

No virtue that America has can ever diminish or vanish; for, virtue is an immortal gift which God Himself grants to aspiring souls and aspiring nations. [95]

∞

The simplicity-mind of a child, the sincerity-heart of a child, the purity-life of a child – only these three things can awaken America. [96]

∞

America does not claim perfection, as far as I can see. America does not claim illumination, as far as I know. Now, does America claim anything? Yes, America does. What does America claim? A colossal preparation: not only for its own illumination and perfection but for the illumination and perfection of the entire world. [97]

∞

Judging by her history, America holds the brightest promise of placing at the service of the Divine her aspirations, aptitudes and capacities, as she has often, in times of need, placed them at the service of humanity. [98]

∞

The American people can better realise their love for the soul of America if they discover that the real and immortal reality in each human being, in each nation, is only the soul-reality. Everything else is transitory. [99]

∞

American politics can return to the spiritual values that they had during the time of the Founding Fathers and some of the previous presidents only if the political leaders and other leaders feel the supreme necessity of an inner life that has the capacity to bring about outer success, outer achievements, outer perfection and outer satisfaction. [100]

Future

Until now the world has seen largely the surfaces of American life, and it has formed its opinion accordingly. Not that her depths have not occasionally come to view, but such occasions have been few in relation to the vastness and variety of her population. Needless to say, there are great indications of a greater future; and as the Hour of God dawns and advances towards its fulness, the splendour of America's soul will show more and more on the surface, even for crude eyes to see. [101]

∞

In the next two hundred years America's contribution to the family of nations will be equality's universal birthright and reality's transcendental height. [102]

∞

America will offer her unprecedented capacity to the community of nations and make all nations feel that her height and depth and speed and power are for them to claim as their very own, and thus create a satisfying and satisfied world-family. [103]

∞

America is great. America is good. America's greatness is going to increase in infinite measure in the next two hundred years because America knows what greatness is and where it comes from. Greatness is self-giving and its source is love in peace and peace in love. America's goodness lies in this: God for God's sake, man for God's sake. Aspiration for a higher life is for God's sake. Truth-discovery is for God's sake. Peace-distribution is for

God's sake. Delight-manifestation is for God's sake. [104]

∞

In her first two hundred years, America learned the momentous necessity of the child-like heart. Now, in order to make the fastest progress, the most important thing is for her to have a life of conscious and continuous self-giving. [105]

∞

There are two special qualities that Americans can work on to help bring forward all their potential divinity. These two divine qualities are the feeling of universal oneness and constant and cheerful self-giving to the Supreme Pilot, who is man's own highest Reality. [106]

∞

Undoubtedly, the spiritual forces will be able to manifest in the next two hundred years much more than they did in the past two hundred years, for not only America's but also humanity's aspiration is continuously proceeding forward, upward and inward. [107]

∞

In the next two hundred years, the citizens of the United States can help themselves develop just by clearing the mind of the thick forest of doubt and by liberating the heart from its insecurity-cave. [108]

∞

American citizens can best further America's role in the world in the next two hundred years by claiming the rest of the world as their very own. This feeling of oneness can alone bring to America an unprecedented leadership and a unique friendship. [109]

∞

When I speak of the United Nations, my mind, heart and soul immediately compel me to speak of the United States in the same breath. When I speak for the United Nations, my mind, heart and soul are immediately blessed by the prosperous and generous soul of the host state – the Empire State – New York.

The term 'united' has always had a special appeal to all human souls, and this transcendent idea has remained in vogue down the sweep of centuries. [110]

∞

To me, the United States and the United Nations are divinely destined to run abreast. Not in vain is the headquarters of the United Nations in the United States – in New York, the capital of the world. This dynamic and fascinating world capital draws the world's attention at every moment. Is there any place that can be more appropriate than New York City to house the vision of universal oneness, which is in the process of being realised and manifested in the heart and soul of humanity?[111]

∞

I admire New York. My eyes are enamoured of her soul's dynamic beauty. My New York is always astir and bustling. Also, she is marching in gigantic strides. Success emerges before her very eyes.

The dawn breaks each day feeling New York's heart consumed with new zeal. She hates to be absorbed in a fog of fruitless brooding and empty inactivity. Moreover, she wants to be free, eternally free. Never within her four corners will she tolerate the air of captivity. If it is part of her nature to express herself boldly, I cannot blame her. To me, first of all, she deserves this acme of self-confidence. And secondly, God wants New York to be what she is.

My New York has courage. My New York has confidence. The problems of anxiety and uncertainty may cover the length and breadth of the world, but my New York is an exception. Her youthful certainty is my heart's delight.

When I think of my India, it seems that she has endless time. If she does not avail herself of an opportunity today, it will return to her tomorrow. But when I think of my New York, it seems that she is facing a unique opportunity at every moment. If she loses a golden opportunity today, it will never return. New York knows how to seize. She knows how to struggle. She knows how to push forward. She knows how to exert herself, consciously and dynamically. Old blunders fail to plague her. Empty of fear is her heart, which ever grows into the fulfilment of her promising future. Blessed is she.

My New York is not a challenge. She is not a competition. She is not a running race. She is not a victory. What then is she? She is a great Promise, wherein grows and flowers the infinite Unknown. [112]

∞

True, at times the United States and the United Nations are not on good terms. But each knows perfectly well that the one adds tremendous value to the other in terms of prestige, recognition, self-awareness and oneness-perfection. Inwardly they know that they truly need and deserve each other.

In silence, unreservedly, the United States gives the United Nations confidence-light. In silence, unreservedly, the United Nations gives the United States oneness-height. Being a seeker, in my silence-heart I feel that the concept of the United Nations has verily come from the United States, unconsciously if not consciously, for the United States had this united feeling two hundred years ago, whereas, the United Nations is only a few decades old. [113]

∞

America says to the United Nations, "Please be careful before you speak." The United Nations says to America, "Please be soulful before you offer." [114]

∞

At the present moment of evolution, the United States says to the United Nations, "If you take my help, you have to use it in my own way."

The United Nations says to the United States, "I am ready to take your help and I shall remain most grateful to you. But if I use your help in your own way, then I will be totally lost in the comity of nations. Whatever you can afford to give me, please give me unconditionally."

The United States immediately responds, "Oh no, I do not want to give you my help unconditionally. I have a right to know whether or not my momentous and generous offering is being utilised properly. As it is my bounden duty to help your supreme cause, O United Nations, I feel that it is also your bounden duty to accept my wisdom-sun on rare occasions."

The United Nations says, "Sorry to stand firm in my belief, O United States. One day you will be blessed with the real joy of unconditional self-giving, which is always without a second."

The inner role of the United Nations amuses the intelligentsia, inspires the world-peace-lovers and nourishes the world-oneness-servers. God has showered His choicest Blessings upon the inner role of the United Nations. When we contemplate the idea of 'role', we immediately think either of responsibility or challenge. But when it is a matter of inner role, there is no such thing as responsibility or challenge; there is only one self-giving Divinity which is breathlessly growing into a self-becoming reality.

The United Nations is often misunderstood. Perhaps its fate will always remain the same. But is there anybody who is not misunderstood, including poor God? Misunderstanding is the order of the day. But that does not and cannot prevent the United Nations from making its soulful self-offering in the creation of a oneness-home for all. [115]

∞

Illumining leaders from all over the world who are serving the United Nations remind us of the undeniable fact that the earth cannot exist without the world-body – the United Nations – in spite of its apparent failings and problems.

The outer role of the United Nations is greatness remarkable. The inner role of the United Nations is goodness admirable. The supreme role of the United Nations is fulness adorable.[116]

∞

The pillars of the United States, its Presidents, call upon us to dedicate ourselves to the most significant cause that the United Nations embodies. Needless to say, the world organisation is God's gracious experiment and precious experience. Such being the case, we must feel an inner obligation to participate in this aspect of God's cosmic Drama. President John F. Kennedy spoke not only to his fellow Americans but to all his fellow beings when he proclaimed:

"My fellow inhabitants of this planet, let us take our stand here in this assembly of nations. And let us see if we, in our own time, can move the world towards a just and lasting peace."

President Carter also powerfully encouraged his country to remain part and parcel of the United Nations. He tells us the true truth that real leadership and continuous service to mankind are inseparable:

"There is no possible means of isolating ourselves from the rest of the world, so we must provide leadership. But this leadership need not depend on our inherent military force, or economic power, or political persuasion. It should derive

*from the fact that we try to be right and honest
and truthful and decent."*

A favourite son of New York, Senator Daniel
Patrick Moynihan, former United States
Ambassador to the United Nations, expressed
his country's sincere awareness of the sublime
necessity of the United Nations:

*"While there have been some calls to boycott
the General Assembly, or not to vote in it, there
have been but few calls for withdrawal from the
United Nations. It is almost as if American opinion now acknowledged that there was no escap-
ing involvement in the emergent world
society."* [117]

∞

A staunch supporter of the United Nations –
indeed, the donor of the land upon which the
U.N. stands – Nelson Rockefeller vividly drew
the parallel between the roots of the United
States and the roots of the United Nations:

*"The federal idea, which our Founding Fathers
applied in their historic act of political creation*

in the eighteenth century, can be applied in
this twentieth century in the larger context of
the world of free nations – if we will but match
our forefathers in courage and vision. The first
historic instance secured freedom and order to
this new nation. The second can decisively serve
to guard freedom and to promote order in a free
world."

As the Declaration of Independence of the
United States is an unparalleled discovery,
even so is the Charter of the United Nations.
The U.S. Declaration of Independence and the
U.N. Charter are humanity's two aspiration-
dedication-realities. The beacon-light of the
Declaration of Independence shows countless
human souls the way to their destined goal:

"We hold these truths to be self-evident, that all
men are created equal, that they are endowed
by their Creator with certain inalienable rights,
that among these are life, liberty and the pur-
suit of happiness, that to secure these rights,
Governments are instituted among men, deriv-
ing their just powers from the consent of the
governed . . ."

The United Nations Charter bravely and heroically proclaims these rights for all of humanity and seeks:

"… to reaffirm faith in fundamental human rights, in the dignity and worth of the human person, in the equal rights of men and women and of nations large and small, and to establish conditions under which justice and respect for the obligations arising from treaties and other sources of international law can be maintained, and to promote social progress and better standards of life in larger freedom." [118]

∞

The composer of the immortal "Hymn to the United Nations", Maestro Don Pablo Casals, reminds us that individuals and their countries undeniably need the United Nations. He gives an inspired call for us to selflessly play our parts in the inner and outer roles of the United Nations:

"Those who believe in the dignity of man should act at this time to bring about a deeper understanding among people and a sincere

rapprochement between conflicting forces. The
United Nations today represents the most impor-
tant hope for peace. Let us give it all power to act
for our benefit. And let us fervently pray that the
near future will disperse the clouds that darken
our days now."

The outer role of the United Nations is a
colossal hope. The inner role of the United
Nations is a generous assurance. The supreme
role of the United Nations is a prosperous
satisfaction.

Hope is a growing plant. Assurance is a
blossoming tree. Satisfaction is a delicious
fruit.

At the present stage, the United Nations is a
growing plant. Is it not absurd for us to expect
the United Nations to solve the overwhelming
problems of centuries? Let the child-plant grow
and glow, smile and cry. Then there shall come
a time when this tiny plant will grow into
a huge tree, with countless leaves, sleepless
flowers and spotless fruits – sheltering, inspiring and nourishing all those who desperately

need its protection-shelter, rejuvenation-inspiration and satisfaction-nourishment. [119]

∞

The American Declaration of Independence had the pioneer vision of faith, dignity and humanity's basic needs: equal rights, justice and freedom. Basically, the same things are found in the Charter of the United Nations. Therefore, we can safely say that the Declaration of Independence and the U.N. Charter are two close friends walking along the same road. One came and joined the other later on the road, and now both are walking together to reach the self-same goal, the goal of world peace and satisfaction. [120]

∞

According to my inner feeling, the United Nations has definitely contributed something very sublime to the consciousness of America. At every moment, the United Nations is aiming at world brotherhood, world peace, world harmony and world oneness. America is undoubtedly the right place for the United Nations to be, for America is constantly offering hope and promise to the world at large. America embodies at once humanity's hope and Divinity's Promise. [121]

∞

The soul of America is promise and the soul of the United Nations is the fulfiller or, you can say, coordinator of that promise. They go together. [122]

∞

The next two hundred years will see the manifestation of the soul's qualities of America. This manifestation will take place in America's conscious and unconditional leadership of humanity and America's constant and self-giving friendship with humanity. [123]

∞

America gained her independence in 1776 by virtue of determined will-power. Now her spiritual independence will be founded upon her conscious oneness with God, and this can be established only on the strength of her implicit surrender to God's divine Dispensation and Will. [124]

∞

America's vision was to become transcendentally great. America's mission is to become universally good. [125]

∞

I feel America has changed for the better . . . What I am seeing now is that each and every human being has a new hope for peace, and this peace-flower is blossoming. Some years ago it was not like that. Today every human being not only feels the necessity of peace, but also feels that peace is something attainable. Before it seemed impossible – it was something to be found only in Heaven.

But today, no matter how many serious mistakes we are making, no matter how much we are quarrelling and fighting, we still feel that there is something called peace and that we can achieve it. We feel something divine and fulfilling is there and that we are being prepared for it. This is the greatest progress that humanity is making, and it is giving me the greatest satisfaction. [126]

∞

When one has run through a very wide range of glittering ephemeral things and sought incessantly to perfect them, one may see a true light from beyond. From this point of view, America has a great possibility of taking to the life of the spirit. This life does not mean withdrawal and inaction, retirement into the forest to give oneself up solely to the contemplation of the Supreme. That kind of isolation is of no avail. The Divine has to be manifested in all His aspects here and now in life. Life itself should be Yoga, union with the Divine; and matter and spirit must go hand in hand.[127]

∞

America's past was God's meaningful promise. America's present is God's soulful cry. America's future will be God's fruitful smile. [128]

∞

Yesterday America enjoyed the sacred flame of
liberty. Today America enjoys the sacred light
of equality. Tomorrow America shall enjoy the
sacred sun of divinity. [129]

∞

America!
You may or may not know what you are doing.
You have conquered matter, but you have kept
it from conquering you. That is why your fund
of scientific knowledge and your bountiful
wealth you freely place at the service of suffering humanity. Another achievement of yours
has been to build up the material basis for the
coming great age of spirituality.

America!
Brought up in the atmosphere of freedom,
you have self-confidence in all your
undertakings.

The benefits of your freedom have fostered in
you a sense of responsibility in all matters of
national and international interest.

America!
Your progressive spirit, striving towards perfection in everything, is a divine blessing. But for your magnanimous participation in many fields of international activity, the world would not be knit together as closely as it is now, though you and the rest of the world have yet a long way to go to reach the destined Goal.

America!
The fairest child of freedom, the first to fight for the divine gift of freedom and win it for the New World. None perhaps has a keener perception of freedom's worth.

America!
The whole freedom-loving world salutes you. The holy flame that burned in your heart when you were smarting under the injustices of imperial domination is still alive in you. Your one single claim to Immortality is this flame. You live not for yourself alone. You live for freedom and for those who share your love for it. [130]

∞

America is wealth.
America is heart.
America is sacrifice.
Before long in America, hopefully,
There will shine forth the world's
    collective soul. [131]

∞

May the infinite beauty
Of America's soul
Awaken America's body,
Liberate America's vital,
Illumine America's mind,
And feed America's heart,
To liberate them from
The fetters of ignorance-night. [132]

Notes

Passages and poems in this volume were excerpted from the sources below. Each source is given an arbitrary alphabetical code to simplify the endnotes. All sources credit Sri Chinmoy with sole authorship.

Sacred Fire, Agni Press, 1975. (Source A)

The Liberty Torch, Agni Press, 1976. (Source B)

The Bicentennial Flames at the United Nations, Agni Press, 1976. (Source C)

I Need My Country: Beauty's Soul, Agni Press, 1975. (Source D)

I Love My Country: Purity's Body, Agni Press, 1975. (Source E)

America in Her Depths, Agni Press, 1973. (Source F)

The World-Experience-Tree-Climber, Part 1, Agni Press, 1986. (Source G)

Sri Chinmoy Answers, Part 1, Agni Press, 1995. (Source H)

George Washington and Thomas Jefferson, an unpublished talk. (Source I)

The Inner Role of the United Nations, Agni Press, 1993. (Source J)

Fifty Freedom-Boats to One Golden Shore, Part 2, Agni Press, 1974. (Source K)

The Seeker's Mind, Agni Press, 1978. (Source L)

Kennedy: The Universal Heart, Agni Press, 1973. (Source M)

Jainism: Give Life, Take Not, Agni Press, 1998. (Source N)

Obedience: A Supreme Virtue, Agni Press, 1977. (Source O)

Mahatma Gandhi: The Heart of Life, Agni Press, 1994. (Source P)

Ten Thousand Flower-Flames, Part 2,
        Agni Press, 1979. (Source Q)

The Golden Boat, Part 18, Agni Press, 1974.
        (Source R)

Choice Wisdom-Fountain-Souls, Agni Press,
        2000. (Source S)

*Twenty-Seven Thousand Aspiration-Plants,
        Part 228*, Agni Press, 1996. (Source T)

Transcendence-Perfection, Agni Press, 1975.
        (Source U)

Sri Chinmoy Answers, Part 18, Agni Press,
        1999. (Source V)

*Aspiration-Suns and Dedication-Moons in My
        Inspiration-Life*, Agni Press, 1998.
        (Source for poem on back cover)

1.	Source A

Prologue

2.	Source B
3.	Source B
4.	Source B
5.	Source B
6.	Source C
7.	Source C
8.	Source C
9.	Source C

Awakening

10.	Source D
11.	Source D
12.	Source D
13.	Source D
14.	Source D
15.	Source D
16.	Source D
17.	Source E
18.	Source E
19.	Source B
20.	Source B
21.	Source D
22.	Source E
23.	Source F
24.	Source E
25.	Source B
26.	Source A
27.	Source A
28.	Source F
29.	Source E
30.	Source G
31.	Source H
32.	Source A

33.	Source I
34.	Source D
35.	Source J

Blossoming

36.	Source D
37.	Source K
38.	Source F
39.	Source D
40.	Source F
41.	Source D
42.	Source D
43.	Source L
44.	Source L
45.	Source L
46.	Source D
47.	Source M
48.	Source M
49.	Source M
50.	Source M
51.	Source M
52.	Source M
53.	Source M
54.	Source N
55.	Source O
56.	Source O
57.	Source O
58.	Source P
59.	Source D
60.	Source F
61.	Source F
62.	Source F
63.	Source F
64.	Source F
65.	Source F
66.	Source F

67.	Source D
68.	Source D
69.	Source J
70.	Source J

Reflections

71.	Source D
72.	Source D
73.	Source D
74.	Source D
75.	Source D
76.	Source C
77.	Source Q
78.	Source B
79.	Source Q
80.	Source R
81.	Source C
82.	Source S
83.	Source C
84.	Source C
85.	Source C
86.	Source U
87.	Source E
88.	Source E
89.	Source E
90.	Source E
91.	Source E
92.	Source E
93.	Source C
94.	Source C
95.	Source J
96.	Source V
97.	Source B
98.	Source F
99.	Source C
100.	Source C

101.	Source F

Future

102.	Source C
103.	Source C
104.	Source C
105.	Source C
106.	Source C
107.	Source C
108.	Source C
109.	Source C
110.	Source J
111.	Source J
112.	Source F
113.	Source J
114.	Source B
115.	Source J
116.	Source J
117.	Source J
118.	Source J
119.	Source J
120.	Source C
121.	Source C
122.	Source C
123.	Source C
124.	Source C
125.	Source B
126.	Source V
127.	Source F
128.	Source B
129.	Source B
130.	Source F
131.	Source F
132.	Source T

Biography of Author

Sri Chinmoy was born in a tiny village in the far eastern region of India (now Bangladesh) on August 27, 1931. His simple, idyllic upbringing in this enclave was nurtured by his loving parents, three elder brothers and three elder sisters. When Sri Chinmoy was eleven, however, his father passed away followed within one year by his mother, abruptly exposing the young boy to excruciating pain and sorrow. The young boy traveled over 1,000 miles away to South India and the Sri Aurobindo Ashram. The Ashram was the epicentre of a spiritual and cultural renaissance led by Sri Aurobindo, the revolutionary-turned-sage, and was where Sri Chinmoy's eldest brother had taken residence some years earlier.

It was in this community that the massive void in the young boy's heart was filled and his unceasing aspiration to understand the roots of human existence was fulfilled through profound experiences of the Infinite.

These colossal realisations of humanity's infinite capacity and ultimate connection to the Supreme drove Sri Chinmoy inward in a journey of blissful self-discovery, where he would remain in deep meditation and contemplation for many hours each day.

Rather than advocate escape from life, the Ashram demanded social interaction and connection to the physical plane. Sri Chinmoy excelled there in a number of capacities, including athletics. A champion sprinter and decathlete as well as a poet and musician, his talents were appreciated far and wide.

In time, however, Sri Chinmoy began to yearn to share his realisation and wisdom with those suffering from the inherent turmoil of life. This aspiration, coupled with a deep admiration for America's ideals and promise, from years of study by great American voices like Jefferson, Emerson, Thoreau and the then-contemporary calls to service of leaders like President John F. Kennedy, drew Sri Chinmoy in 1964, aged 32, to the heart of New York City.

Over the next forty years, Sri Chinmoy's life of service blossomed and found a home in the hearts of many. From meetings with world leaders and leading meditations at the United Nations and other august institutions to offering 700 free musical concerts for peace and launching initiatives that reached millions such as the World Harmony Run, Sri Chinmoy's work inspired people the world over.

An incredibly prolific artist and man of culture, Sri Chinmoy lovingly and painstakingly created a collection of works of staggering quantity. At the same time, he strived through his creative work to illumine the heart, to lift his audience above the trials and tribulations of life and to give them a hint of their own significant role in the universe.

A poet and writer since his childhood, Sri Chinmoy composed over 120,000 poems and published more than 1,500 literary works, including prose, poetry, plays and lectures he has given at the United Nations and at major universities, such as Harvard, Cambridge, Oxford and Yale.

His poems range from brief two-line aphorisms, often compared to ancient Sanskrit sutras in the depth conveyed in disarming simplicity, to masterpieces of modernity. His writing evokes a sense of humanity's interconnectedness and invokes a deeper feeling of personal responsibility.

Sri Chinmoy received a number of honorary doctorate degrees, as well as numerous accolades and citations from major universities worldwide.

Sri Chinmoy passed away on October 11, 2007 at his home in New York City. The Sri Chinmoy Centre continues his work through its presence in over 40 nations.

Praise Offered During Sri Chinmoy's Lifetime

"Your deeds are invaluable, for they cannot be measured by any economic or political parameters. They are noble and cure the human soul."
– President Mikhail Gorbachev

"It is a very rare gift indeed for humankind to be blessed with such a selfless individual who has dedicated his entire life to the service of world peace … Your work has inspired spiritual growth, resilience and well-being, especially in view of the present and unprecedented onslaughts against humankind … Yours is a voice of reason that we must all heed."
– President Nelson Mandela

"All that you are doing for the world is for the Glory of God and the good of people! Pray for me as I pray for you and for all of your many projects for world peace. Your works of love are works of prayer, and your works of prayer are works of God."
– Mother Teresa

Special thanks to Dr. James Basker, Ms. Karen Coviello, the staff of the Manifestation-Glow Printing Press, and the Sri Chinmoy Centre.

Please visit www.illumine.com/press for information on other editions by Illumine Press.

Kindly visit www.srichinmoy.org for more information on Sri Chinmoy.